Original title:
Tropical Fruit Dreams

Copyright © 2025 Creative Arts Management OÜ
All rights reserved.

Author: Evan Hawthorne
ISBN HARDBACK: 978-1-80586-365-6
ISBN PAPERBACK: 978-1-80586-837-8

The Celestial Garden of Kiwi

In a garden where kiwis glow,
They dance with the wind, putting on a show.
With fuzzy coats and a wink so sly,
They giggle and bounce, oh my, oh my!

Pineapples wear hats, so tall and bright,
Mangoes debate if they're yellow or light.
Bananas slip on their peels with grace,
While coconuts drop in a clumsy race.

The dragonfruit's tales are wild and grand,
Claiming it once did a jig on the sand.
Papayas chuckle at the sun's warm beam,
Together they plot a grand fruity dream.

In this garden so absurd yet sweet,
The fruits throw a party, oh what a treat!
With laughter and juice flowing like streams,
Every day here feels like the wildest dreams!

Slices of Sunshine

In the land of juicy bites,
Bananas wear their hats quite tight.
Pineapples dance on sunny days,
While mangoes giggle in their rays.

Coconuts roll, they play and spin,
While limes are trying to fit in.
Oranges juggle with their zest,
Slicing through laughter, they're the best!

Papaya Dreams on the Horizon

Papayas float on fluffy clouds,
Wearing smiles that draw big crowds.
Kiwi sings a silly tune,
Underneath a bright, round moon.

Lemons throw confetti bright,
As fruit folks join the silly fight.
They pit their puns with fruity flair,
In a zesty world beyond compare.

Cherries Beneath a Starlit Canopy

Cherries giggle in the night,
While raspberries glow in soft moonlight.
Grapes gather round to share a joke,
Making fruity mischief as they poke.

Plums are dressed in purple hues,
Playing pranks with all their views.
Under stars, the fruits unite,
Creating laughter, pure delight!

Fields of Fruit Fantasies

In colorful fields where fruits take flight,
Strawberries whisper, 'What a sight!'
Pears play tag and leap quite high,
While blueberries giggle as they fly.

Watermelons roll with laughter loud,
Creating chaos in their crowd.
Each fruit shares a tale so bold,
In this silly realm of sweet and gold!

Memories of Mango Tango

In a land where palms sway high,
Mangoes dance and wink an eye.
When the sun begins to dip,
I chase them down, a fruity trip.

At parties, they spin on plates,
In fruity hats, they love their fates.
I grab one and it starts to giggle,
With every slice, my heart does wiggle.

Nectarine Nights and Kiwi Days

Nectarines glow like evening stars,
I squeeze them tight, they smell like cars.
On summer nights, we toast with cheer,
The juiciest bites, oh dear, oh dear!

Kiwi fuzz tickles my nose,
A green surprise in fruity prose.
With every taste, I laugh and sprawl,
These wacky fruits will have a ball!

Papaya Promises in the Breeze

Papayas whisper secrets sweet,
Underneath the warm sun's heat.
Harvest time, we have a parade,
Silly hats and shades are made.

As breezes blow, they sway and tease,
With giggles floating on the breeze.
I trip and tumble in their cheer,
This fruity fun can't disappear!

A Chorus of Colorful Cherimoya

Cherimoya sings a fruity tune,
In my garden beneath the moon.
With voices sweet and laughter bright,
They serenade the soft twilight.

Colorful dreams in every bite,
They play hide and seek at night.
With each scoop, I laugh and play,
Cherimoya keeps the blues at bay!

Sugar-Sweet Serenade

Oh, the banana danced with glee,
In pajamas, sipping lemonade tea.
Mangoes wore hats, quite a sight,
While berries had a berry-good night.

A pineapple played the ukulele,
As the grapes wiggled, oh so frilly.
Lemons laughed in the lemon-sun,
Squeezed their juice, oh what fun!

Mango Moonlit Whispers

Mangoes twinkled under the stars,
Wearing tiny little guitars.
They strummed their tunes to the night,
While avocados took flight!

Limes rolled down from the moon,
Singing a zesty, lively tune.
Coconuts joined with a cheer,
Dropping jokes, what a funny sphere!

Papaya Winds and Coconut Skies

Papayas giggled as they spun,
In the breeze, they had such fun.
Coconuts swung with all their might,
Chasing rainbows, feeling bright!

A pineapple wore a lovely crown,
In a fashion show, it won the town.
Kiwi slid on a fruity slide,
Out of control, what a wild ride!

The Lush Embrace of Pineapple

In the garden, where sunflowers beam,
Pineapples giggle, living the dream.
Coconuts juggle, laugh, and roll,
While melons plot their dancing goal.

Grapes held a party, oh what a bash,
Stomping on feet, causing a crash.
Peaches tossed confetti in the air,
With fruity laughter everywhere!

The Sugary Lull of Palm Trees

Beneath the swaying palms we play,
With coconuts wearing hats all day.
Laughter dances on the breeze,
As we sip juice, oh, if you please!

A parrot joins with jokes so bright,
Doing stand-up, what a sight!
Mangoes roll and giggle near,
While pineapple dudes cheer, oh dear!

Whispering Mango Mysteries

Mangoes whisper secrets sweet,
Like gossip queens with juicy meat.
They tell of love and sticky hands,
In a land of fruit where fun expands.

Lime joins in with zesty flair,
Cracking jokes, without a care.
Bananas slip, oh what a fall,
As everyone laughs, they're having a ball!

Golden Sun and Grape

In the sunshine, grapes all shine,
Wearing shades and sipping brine.
They laugh at how they roll around,
In this fruity circus, joy is found.

Berry buddies toast with cheer,
Sipping nectar, oh so dear.
Underneath the sun's warm glance,
They dance in a silly grape romance!

Figs under the Starry Sky

Figs in pajamas, ready for bed,
Telling stories 'bout what they said.
Under stars, they giggle and leap,
While dreaming of treats from dreams so deep.

A fig says, "I'm sweet as pie!"
Another dreams of flying high.
"Let's start a band!" they cheer with glee,
A fruity concert—come and see!

A Dance of Sweet Tamarind Tales

In the trees, the tamarind swings,
With laughter, its sourness sings.
Monkeys wear hats, they shimmy and sway,
A fruity fiesta, all night and day.

Charming the kids with its twisty grin,
Sticky fingers and juice that spins.
Each bite a giggle, each taste a cheer,
Spilling secrets only friends can hear.

Cherries from the Island of Echoes

Cherries bouncing on waves of sound,
Whispers of laughter all around.
They play hide and seek in the sun,
With juicy jokes, oh, what fun!

Each cherry pops like a tiny joke,
Rolling away with a teasing poke.
On a sandy shore, they gather to cheer,
A fruit parade, we all draw near.

Luscious Lemons in the Sun

Lemons wearing shades, so bold and bright,
Sipping sunshine, what a sight!
They crack up jokes with their zesty flair,
Spraying giggles everywhere!

In lemonade rivers, they frolic and play,
Sour and sweet, the best of the day.
They dance on tables, they twirl and spin,
Heartfelt laughter, let the fun begin!

A Cascade of Fruitful Fantasies

Pineapples wear crowns, they rule the land,
Creating a kingdom, oh so grand.
Bouncing bananas join in the dance,
With every slip, they take a chance.

In this realm of fruity delight,
Every flavor shines, oh what a sight!
Silly smoothies flow like streams,
Together they weave hilarious dreams.

Papaya's Sweet Embrace

In the sun, a papaya grins,
With orange skin and squishy sins,
It wobbles like a jelly treat,
Inviting all for fruity feats.

A squirrel tried to take a bite,
But slipped and fell, what a sight!
With laughter rippling through the leaves,
The papaya just sways, and believes.

Beneath the Banana Palms

Bananas swing on lazy trees,
A dance of yellow in the breeze,
They whisper jokes, oh what a scene,
Saying, "Hey, where's that monkey bean?"

A vine tangled in such delight,
A monkey yells, "This won't be right!"
He slips and lands, a fruity mess,
And laughs, proclaiming, "I must confess!"

Lush Harvest of the Islands

Mangos roll on golden shores,
Like tiny suns that sing in roars,
With every bite, a juicy joke,
Revealing sweetness, laughter woke.

Coconuts bounce with merry cheer,
Claiming, "Crack me open, come near!"
They giggle as they spin and whirl,
While sipping drinks with a fun swirl.

Celestial Pineapple Nights

Pineapples twinkle in the dark,
Their crowns like stars, each a spark,
They dream of parties, wild and bright,
With hula dancers, pure delight.

One pineapple stomped his feet,
Declared, "Come join, this is the beat!"
The others laughed and swayed along,
Beneath the moon, they sang their song.

Starfruit Skylines

In a land of twinkling stars,
Where fruit had funny bars,
Starfruits danced on clouds so bright,
Wearing hats of pure delight.

Bananas laughed, they slipped and spun,
The giggles echo, so much fun,
Pineapples with their crowns held high,
Swayed to tunes that made them fly.

Coconuts rolled with silly glee,
Debating who could climb the tree,
In this fruity, zany place,
Joyful laughter leaves a trace.

So here's to skies of fruit and fun,
Under the bright and cheerful sun,
Where every bite brings laughs anew,
And silly dreams for me and you.

Raspberry Reflections

In a mirror of juicy bliss,
Raspberries give a cheeky kiss,
Reflecting smiles, round and sweet,
They waltz around on tiny feet.

Jellybean bees buzz by in cheer,
Stirring up giggles, oh so near,
While apples snicker in their core,
Saying, 'We're not fruit, we're lore!'

Pies with legs run down the street,
Chasing after little feet,
Raspberry dreams swirl in a dance,
Hoping for that second chance.

So raise a toast with fruity juice,
To reflections that let us choose,
To laugh and play, just like a mime,
In raspberry dreams, we waste no time.

Plumeria Blossom Lullaby

In a garden full of giggles bright,
Plumeria blooms sing at night,
They tease the moon to dance along,
With petals soft and pure as song.

The breeze can't help but sway and sway,
As flowers chuckle, come what may,
While fireflies blink with silly winks,
Painting tales that make you think.

A watering can tells a joke,
To every leaf, it's quite the poke,
The plumeria's laugh fills the air,
Whispers tickle, without a care.

So close your eyes, let petals twirl,
In this world of laughter swirl,
A lullaby of laughter sweet,
With every bloom, we find our beat.

The Mango Tango

Mangoes in a party dress,
Twirl around, it's such a mess,
They take a sip of sunny cheer,
And tango with the waves so near.

Lemons squeeze in, throwing shade,
As mangoes grooved with their parade,
Lime, the DJ, spins the tunes,
While cherries dance beneath the moons.

Fruit salads join, in ranks they prance,
Mixing flavors in a dance,
Coconuts on the sidelines cheer,
Laughing hard, they hold their beer.

So let's all join this fruit ballet,
In a swirl of color, bright and gay,
For in this juicy, silly scene,
Life is a dance on the fruit machine.

Figs Beneath a Silken Sky

Figs dance in the warm sunlight,
Wearing cloaks of purple delight.
Squirrels plot with tiny glee,
To steal a nibble, oh wee!

Bees buzz like they own the place,
Chasing shadows, a frantic race.
With each wiggle, a giggling spree,
Underneath the fig tree, we're free.

A sliding lizard joins the feast,
Grinning wide, it's quite the beast.
With every bite, a juicy splash,
Watch out! Here comes a slippery dash!

Laughter echoes in the shade,
As fruit-filled dreams start to cascade.
Let's toast to this wacky array,
Under the figs, we laugh and play!

Exotic Ecstasy of Rambutan Ride

On a rambling, bumpy street,
Rambutans roll, oh what a treat!
Fuzzy balls with a squishy grin,
Join the ride, let the fun begin!

Bouncing high, they bounce off walls,
Making friends with funky calls.
They play hopscotch with the sun,
Chasing shadows, oh what fun!

Our laughter mixes with the breeze,
As rambutans dance with such ease.
Their wild antics, a glorious sight,
In this fruity, joyous flight!

So grab a bunch and hold on tight,
For this Rambutan ride feels so right.
A merry feast, a playful cheer,
With every bounce, we have no fear!

The Garden of Melon Murmurs

In a garden where melons talk,
With giggles stemming from each stalk.
Watermelons play peek-a-boo,
While cantaloupes sing just for you.

Honeydews whisper sweet secrets,
Spilling tales of juicy regrets.
"Don't eat me first!" a seedling cries,
"I'm the star of all BBQs and pies!"

Melons roll in a friendly race,
With berry buddies keeping pace.
They twirl and spin, causing a scene,
In this garden, laughter's routine.

So wield your fork and take a bite,
In this garden, everything's bright.
For in every slice, a giggle hides,
Among the melons, joy abides!

Artistry in Fleshy Fruits

Artisans in a juicy show,
Crafting art with a citrus glow.
Papayas paint with sunset hues,
While pineapples wear vibrant shoes.

A mango winks, "Come take a taste!"
Swirling flavors done with haste.
Each slice a canvas, bold and bright,
In this fruity, tasty sight!

Bananas juggle with great flair,
Bouncing laughter into the air.
In this circus, all fruits unite,
Creating giggles, pure delight!

So grab a fork and taste the art,
In each sweet bite, joy plays a part.
Crafted with humor, crafted with care,
In the world of fruits, laughter's everywhere!

Soft Caresses of Soursop Sleep

A soursop sighs in the moonlit night,
Coconuts giggle, oh what a sight!
Pineapples dance with the breeze so sweet,
As bananas waltz on their little green feet.

Mangoes snicker, they can't contain,
They mimic the words of a sleepy train.
Lychees chuckle, ticking clocks fall,
As the starfruit sings, it's a free-for-all.

Failing to nap, the dreamers tease,
A papaya whispers with rustling leaves.
In the realm where these fruits do prance,
Everything's silly; it's a grand romance.

Who knew these fruits had such a flair?
A ripe delight, floating in the air.
As the night wears on, they throw a fest,
Soft caresses of soursop, what a quest!

Harvesting Dreams from Frosted Pines.

In icy realms where the pine trees sway,
Fruit conspire to have their way.
Frost-laden berries, giggle and shout,
In a winter game, there's no doubt.

Peaches peer through the snowflakes grim,
Cherries chase dreams on a frosty whim.
With every pluck, there's more to share,
Laughter erupts, filling the air.

Kiwi glees at the frozenness bright,
Engaging the warmth of the glowing light.
As the sun creeps in with a cheeky grin,
Frost melts away, let the fun begin!

Harvesting laughter with every bite,
If fruit could giggle, oh what a sight!
They dash through fields, with all their might,
Painting dreams under the starlit night.

Sunset Citrus Serenade

Lemons strum on a zesty guitar,
While oranges croon from near and far.
In sunset hues, the fruits unite,
A citrus serenade in the fading light.

Limes are juggling, hopping round,
With zest in their hearts, they leap from the ground.
The tangerines twist, they can't let go,
As grapefruit rolls in for the show.

As the sky blushes in pink delight,
The fruits start dancing, feeling just right.
With every beat, they giggle and spin,
Creating a rhythm, let the fun begin!

Singing sweet songs under the stars,
Mangoes float by, playing guitars.
Beneath the twilight, they take their stand,
In the sunset glow, they form a band!

Mango Whispers in the Breeze

Mangoes talk secrets in rustling trees,
Tickling the air with a mischievous tease.
Papayas giggle, they can hardly stand,
While coconuts chill with a drink in hand.

Pineapples plot behind leafy screens,
Sharing their tales of sweet, juicy dreams.
Each whispering breeze carries their cheer,
As laughter erupts, it's a fruity frontier!

Bananas banter in yellow attire,
With a comedic flair that climbs even higher.
As fruit flies giggle, they share a laugh,
Drawing us all into their fruity path.

Remember to savor the tropical glee,
With mangoes and friends, oh, what a spree!
In the winds of joy, the echoes release,
Mango whispers floating in blissful peace.

Sapodilla Secrets

In the shade a fruit does hide,
A secret sweet on nature's side.
With a grin it comes to play,
Whispers tales of sunny day.

Its skin is rough, like a million laughs,
Slicing through it, just like gaffs.
Inside, the sweetness makes you hum,
A party waiting, oh so fun!

Each bite a giggle, every drop a cheer,
Inviting friends, come gather near.
Let's make a feast, let worries flee,
In sapodilla's world, we're all so free!

So grab a fruit, let's dance and swing,
With this delight, we're the fruit king.
A pocket of joy, tucked in the skin,
In sapodilla's realm, let the fun begin!

Euphoria in Every Bite

With bananas dressed in polka dots,
We host a party in sunny spots.
Split them open, let's take a look,
And dive right into this funky book.

Mango tango, do the groove,
The juicy beats make us all move.
Swinging from branches, laughter flows,
In every slice, sweet chaos grows.

A pit inside, like a little gem,
Oh this fruit, where do I begin?
Each bite a tickle, each taste a laugh,
A fruity carnival in this lovely path.

So gather round with smiles so bright,
Let's munch and munch, from morning to night.
With joy unchained, there's no need to fight,
In this fruity realm, everything feels right!

Calm After the Storm of Kiwis

A storm of kiwis rains down fun,
With fuzzy skins, oh what a run!
Each slice a green, delightful cheer,
Who knew storms could bring such sheer?

We swim in fruit like it's the sea,
Splashing sweetness, wild and free.
A tiny army, they line the plate,
With curious looks, they captivate.

The tartness tickles, the sweetness sings,
In every fruit bowl, joy takes wing.
Let's gather the troops for a buttercup,
With kiwis all around, we'll never give up!

Amidst the breezes, laughter ignites,
Cracking jokes as the kiwi bites.
From stormy squalls, we find the calm,
In fruity splashes, we raise our palm!

Mandarins in the Mist

Mandarins peel, like a jester's jest,
Rolling and tumbling, they do their best.
In misty mornings, orange delight,
Bringing laughter to every bite.

Tiny spheres with a citrus song,
A merry crew, we all belong.
With juicy bursts, they dance and play,
In every zest, our woes decay.

A squirt of bliss, oh what a game,
In this world, nothing's the same.
We build our castles, citrus-sweet,
Where every moment is a fruity treat.

So gather round in the morning light,
Mandarins calling us to unite.
With laughter and fun, we'll raise a fist,
In the misty cheer, we simply can't resist!

Guava Hues in Twilight

In twilight's glow, guavas dance bright,
With giggles and giggles, oh what a sight!
Fruits in a frenzy, like a wild ballet,
Swinging their colors, come join the play!

Lemonade laughter, they squirt with glee,
Winking and twirling, come sip with me.
Pineapple atop like a crown so proud,
While cherries cheer loud, a merry crowd!

A mango with jokes, oh what a tease,
Whispers sweet secrets, brings friends to their knees.
In this fruity fiesta, all smiles abound,
In the hue of the night, joy knows no bounds!

So gather your buddies, let's feast tonight,
On laughter and colors, in fading light.
With guava hues swirling, we'll dance till we drop,
In the heart of the twilight, the fun never stops!

Juicy Paradiso

A splash of zesty, the berries parade,
With giggling melons that never fade.
Papaya pops out with a grin so wide,
In this juicy paradise, let's take a ride!

Kiwi and mango, a duo so sweet,
Creating a world where laughter can't beat.
Peaches are plotting their next big scheme,
Crafting a whirlpool of a juicy dream!

In the shade of the orchard, the fun multiplies,
Grapes fumble and tumble, oh what a surprise!
With each fruit a jester, a flavoric play,
In this realm of delights, come join the fray!

So roll up your sleeves and take a big bite,
In the juicy paradiso, everything feels right.
With fruit on our faces, we laugh and we sing,
In this vibrant fair, we're the fruity king!

The Lychee's Secret Garden

In a garden of mysteries, lychee stands shy,
Wearing a coat of pink underneath the sky.
With whispers of sweetness, it beckons so bold,
Join the laughter in stories untold!

Under the branches, where dreams take flight,
Cabbage and carrots can't join the delight.
While fruits make a fuss, frolicking free,
The lychee's giggles echo like glee!

The cacti are thorns, but what do they know?
In this fruity mischief, it's all about flow.
A hop and a skip, a wink and a tease,
The lychee's secret garden is sure to please!

So pluck off a treasure, take a peek inside,
In the giggles of fruit, together we glide.
With laughter entwined, we munch on the fun,
In this garden of sweetness, we joyfully run!

Coconut Breaths of Summer

Coconuts crack jokes with a swaying grin,
Sipping on sunshine, let the fun begin!
With sandy foot taps and a wave of flair,
Inside every shell, summer's bold air!

The ocean hums tunes of a salty beat,
While coconut palms tap dance on our feet.
Their laughter cascades with each breeze so light,
As we sway 'neath the stars, oh what a sight!

Mangoes do handstands, all merry and bright,
Enticing the coconuts to join the flight.
In breezy delights, there's no room for frowns,
Underneath the sun, joy wears all the crowns!

So fill up your glasses, let's toast to this glee,
With coconut breaths, we'll treasure the spree.
In summer's embrace, let the giggles unfold,
In this whimsical land, where laughter is gold!

Between Fruit and Fantasy

In a land where bananas wear hats,
A melon strums tunes with playful spats.
Pineapples dance on the beach at night,
While mangoes twirl in sheer delight.

Coconut cups are filled with cheer,
As guavas whisper secrets near.
Rambutans giggle, making a scene,
In this dreamland where fruits are keen.

Limes wear shades, looking so cool,
Lemonade rivers flow to a pool.
Kiwi kites fly high in the sky,
While oranges laugh as they roll by.

Here, the fruitcakes don't have a stake,
Instead, they dance and bake a cake.
In a world where flavors explode,
Every fruit tells a story so bold.

Citrus Cascade of Colour

Lemons bounce like little suns,
While oranges play their fruity puns.
Limes juggle jokes, with zest they share,
In a citrus world beyond compare.

Tangerines trot in polka-dot shoes,
Grapefruits giggle, spread the news.
The rainbow spills upon leafy beds,
As candied laughter tickles our heads.

Clementines giggle, they just can't stop,
While key limes twirl on a candy shop.
Sour cherries cheer in a sweet parade,
With every peel, new fun is made.

Lime trees sway with a fruity swing,
As poppies dance, their petals bring.
In this citrus cascade, joy's supreme,
Life's a punchline, a fruity dream.

Dreams Wrapped in Foliage

Under green leaves, the party starts,
With cocoa nibs and sweet nut hearts.
A jackfruit sings a lullaby,
While berries paint the clouds up high.

Papayas float like boats on streams,
As spiky durians plot their schemes.
Veggies join the flavorful ball,
Tomatoes blush beneath it all.

Chili peppers give some fiery cheer,
While leafy greens whistle songs we hear.
In this garden where laughter thrives,
Every bite raises the fun that vibes.

Wrapped in foliage, dreams take flight,
Beneath the sun, all feels just right.
In this world, let go of your dread,
Taste the joy, let it spread!

Paprika and Papaya

Paprika twirls in a salsa of fun,
While papayas hide, feeling quite done.
They giggle and laugh in the pantry's light,
As sweet fragrances mix in delight.

Chili dances with a fruity shimmy,
While green apples watch, feeling quite whimsy.
In a pot where spices gather and greet,
Each blend tells a story that's hard to beat.

Cucumbers crunch while tomatoes cheer,
As peppers come in to lend an ear.
Together in chaos, joy's the main dish,
Each bite is a dream, a tasty wish.

So slice up those colors, let flavors unfold,
In this saucy adventure, be brave and bold.
Paprika and papaya, a duo divine,
Where laughter and spices together align.

When Fruit Becomes Poetry

A pineapple wrote a sonnet, so sweet,
With verses so juicy, a tasty treat.
Mangoes danced on the table with glee,
While bananas debated, 'Who's funnier, me?'

The oranges sang, in a zesty choir,
Limes chimed in, setting their hopes higher.
Grapes giggled softly, in their purple suit,
Dreaming of riding a grand fruit parade route.

Coconuts came, in their tough but vain shell,
Claiming their stories were savory and swell.
Pomegranates plucked out the seeds of delight,
As cherries just blushed in the tropical night.

Lemons with laughter, a sour twist rhyme,
Squeezed all their punch in an ode to the time.
This banquet of verses, oh how it gleams,
Each line a burst, in our fruity daydreams.

The Lushness of Limes

In a lime grove under the sun's bright rays,
Sour green jesters perform silly plays.
They skip and they roll, with zest on their side,
A comedy of flavors, they simply can't hide.

Juicy jests flow from their citrusy lips,
Spinning wild tales of their tangy trips.
A lime in a bowler hat, oh so refined,
Sips a smoothie, questioning what's truly aligned.

"Why do we limes seem so often ignored?"
A pondering fruit on a tart, fruity board.
But laughter erupts from the zesty brigade,
Who shake up the world in a lime-laden parade.

So here's to the limes, in their green, playful glory,
Whose antics and jests tell the best fruity story.
Together they whirl, in a jest and a rhyme,
Making life zesty, one laugh at a time.

Hibiscus Hues and Flavors

Hibiscus petals in colors so bright,
Twist in a dance on a warm, breezy night.
With laughter they flutter, a floral charade,
Trying to steal all the sun's luscious shade.

Each sip of their nectar, a crafty delight,
Whispering secrets all through the night.
Brewed into teas, they giggle and tease,
As aromas are swirling, like a fragrant breeze.

"Who's the fairest?" the petals all shout,
With a splash of cold water, they whirl about.
They dream of their colors in wild, wavy streams,
In gardens of laughter and caffeine-fueled dreams.

Oh, the fun in a flower that blooms just for tea,
With each little sip, it's bright jubilee.
Forget all your worries, just savor the sight,
Of hibiscus hues dancing in gentle moonlight.

Gardens of the Golden Guava

In gardens where the golden guava grows,
The fruit jests and plays, as everyone knows.
They wear tiny crowns, embracing their flair,
With giggles and splashes, they sprinkle good air.

The wise old guava, with stories galore,
Talks of adventures from seasons before.
He chuckles at rumors of fruit salad fame,
Yet loves little parties, where all bring their game.

With smoothies and snacks, the fun starts anew,
While guavas debate if kiwi is true blue.
Inevitably, laughter and juice fill the space,
In this garden of whimsy, sweet fruits interlace.

So join in the jubilee, taste joy all around,
The golden guava's magic simply abounds.
Ready your forks, and let's make a toast,
To gardens of laughter, we cherish the most!

The Juicy Echo of Sapodilla

In a land where sapodillas grow,
A monkey slipped on the fruit, oh no!
He landed right in a mango's shade,
And dreamed of a juice parade.

With laughter all around the trees,
A parrot squawked in the gentle breeze.
"Why is this fruit so sweet and round?"
The monkey grinned without a sound.

They danced upon a fruity stage,
While ants lined up to join the rage.
Each bite brought giggles, oh-so-fine,
The sapodilla's a funny design!

So if you trip on a juicy treat,
Just roll with it; it'll be quite neat.
A fruit-filled life, a silly tale,
Where laughter's juice will never fail.

Coconut Waters and Coral Shores

Upon the sand, we take a sip,
From coconuts, we never trip.
With straws like snorkels, laughter flies,
As we chase crabs who wear disguise.

The waves come in with a splashy cheer,
While sea turtles dance without any fear.
I yelled, "Hey, watch out for that float!"
But the turtle gave me a humorous gloat.

Coconut water rains like fun,
As sunburned faces start to run.
We toss our shells to a distant shore,
But they boomerang back; oh, what a score!

So bring your shades and your goofy hats,
Let's sip and giggle with friendly chats.
In this beachy paradise, we'll be free,
Chasing sunsets with glee and glee!

Whispered Secrets of the Dragonfruit

A dragonfruit with scales so bright,
Whispers secrets in the night.
"Why am I purple? Is that a dream?"
The fruit said, blotting the moonbeam.

With spiky crowns and a juicy core,
It rolled away, then back for more.
"Every slice is a riddle, you see,
I'm the king of fruits, bow down to me!"

But when it tripped on a berry's hue,
It fell in laughter, shouting, "Who knew?"
With smirks, the fruit started to dance,
Creating a fruity, silly romance.

So lend your ears to this fuzzy plight,
For fruit can giggle, and that's alright.
In the garden, let joy take flight,
With whispered secrets shared each night.

Lychee Lullabies in Summer's Glow

Under the stars, where lychees sing,
A giggling breeze takes flight on a wing.
Each bite's like candy, sweet and round,
With laughter spilling on the ground.

As summer glows with laughter's tune,
Lychees argue who's the cutest fruit of June.
"Look at my fuzz, and oh, my red skin!"
But the mango winked, "Where do I begin?"

They swayed in the moonlight's warm embrace,
Trying to win the fruitiest race.
"Oh no! I've slipped; it's a fruity flop!"
And giggles echoed until they'd stop.

With lullabies made of zest and cheer,
The fruits unite, making fun quite clear.
So gather round for a fruity tale,
Where laughter's sweetness will always prevail.

Wanderlust in Watermelon

A slice so juicy, oh what a treat,
Travel the world with every sweet bite.
Hitch a ride on a juicy seed,
Adventure awaits, with every delight.

A picnic basket, the sun's shining bright,
Watermelon boats sail, oh what a sight!
With laughter and giggles, we splash all around,
In this funny fruit kingdom, joy knows no bound.

Sipping juice oceans, as waves hit the shore,
Each gulp a journey, who could want more?
With seeds like confetti, we toss in the air,
Landing on laughter, floating without a care.

So grab a fork, let the laughter erupt,
In this fruity fiesta, we're all plump and cupped.
From rind to the center, our laughter it beams,
All aboard the whimsy, on watermelon dreams!

Ambrosia of the Tropics

An exotic bowl of colors to munch,
With pineapple winks and a sly little crunch.
Banana boats sail on a coconut sea,
Dancing with mangoes, oh what glee!

Sticky fingers diving into sweet delight,
Passionfruit giggles, oh what a sight!
The papayas whisper secrets so grand,
As the laughter erupts like waves on the sand.

One chutney, two chutneys, all piled so high,
Fruit salad shenanigans—oh me, oh my!
Citrus confetti raining like dreams,
We tuck in our napkins and mix up our schemes.

In this ambrosial chaos, we risk a good mess,
Every bite taken, we taste and confess.
Fruitful adventures, an insatiable quest,
To find joy in flavors, we're truly blessed!

The Secret Orchard

Hidden beneath the mango trees,
Laughter echoes with each gentle breeze.
Papayas jiggle, the coconuts sway,
In this secret orchard, we frolic and play.

Grapefruit giggles bounce off the walls,
Limes in sunglasses doing funny falls.
Beneath twinkling stars, the fruit comes alive,
As we dance with the melons, oh how they thrive!

Pineapples whisper, "Join us today!"
Bounce on the buncha, let worries decay.
In a realm of sweetness, whimsy's unchained,
Sipping on nectar where craziness reigned.

So grab all your friends and spin in delight,
In this secret spot, every wrong feels right.
With juicy adventures, the night never ends,
In laughter and fruit, we're the best of friends!

Cherries in the Moonlight

Under the moon's glimmer, cherries take flight,
Swinging on branches, oh what a sight.
Their laughter echoes through the starry vale,
As they giggle and tumble, leaving a trail.

In a whimsical dance, they twirl and they spin,
Petals are confetti, the party begins!
"Oh dear," says a cherry, "I'm stuck on this vine!
Help me escape—oh, it's fruit-picking time!"

With every mischief, a wink and a cheer,
Fruitful adventures kick off, never fear!
In the moonlit orchard, we'll laugh till we drop,
Under cherry trees, we'll never stop.

So gather your friends for a juicy good laugh,
In this funny fruit kingdom, we'll write our own path.
Cherries in the moonlight, let's giggle and sway,
In a whimsically fruity, delightful ballet!

Whispered Wishes of Pomegranates

In a garden bright and sweet,
Where pomegranates dare to meet,
They giggle with their ruby glow,
Wishing for a dance, you know!

Each seed a joke, they laugh out loud,
As nectar drips, they draw a crowd,
A fruity showdown, just for fun,
With bursts of laughter, they outrun.

So grab a bowl and join the feast,
Where flavors clash and joy increased,
In every bite a chuckle plays,
As crimson smiles light up our days.

They whisper secrets, sweet and queer,
About the time a squirrel came near,
He tried to snack, but lost his grip,
Now joins the dance, this juicy trip!

The Sweet Echoes of Nature

Mangoes hanging in the sun,
Chasing shadows, just for fun,
They boast of sweetness, soft and round,
While parrots mimic all around.

A peach once slipped, and rolled away,
It laughed, escaping the cliché,
While coconut clinks an empty shell,
Joining the prattle, all is well.

Bananas swing from leafy heights,
Throwing parties on starry nights,
Their peels create a slip-and-slide,
Where giggles turn to fruit-filled pride.

Grapes create a wobbly train,
Chugging cheer through juicy lanes,
Each laugh a wave, a fruity sound,
An echo of delight abound.

Beyond the Orchard

Beyond the trees, where laughter grows,
A papaya in a silly pose,
With sunglasses on, it strikes a pose,
In the sunny air, anything goes!

A pineapple in a top hat waits,
Claiming it's the king of fates,
While lemons jiggle, dance with flare,
It's a fruity ball, beyond compare!

Figs tease with tales of wild dreams,
While cherries burst with giggly screams,
A secret club of fruity cheer,
Where juicy jokes are always near.

Watermelons roll and spin,
With every twist, they wear a grin,
Beyond the orchard, fun prevails,
In nature's rhythm, laughter sails!

A Symphony of Sweetness

In the land of syrup and cheer,
Fruits form an orchestra so dear,
With lychee plucking harp strings bright,
Their melody brings pure delight.

Citrus chimes with every squeeze,
Creating tunes that aim to please,
While berries beat the drums in time,
A rhythm of fun, simply sublime.

Kiwi joins with a quirky song,
Encouraging the rest along,
Together they perform with zest,
A fruity fest, that's simply best!

With every bite, the joy ascends,
In harmony, the laughter blends,
A sweet symphony, oh what a scene,
In a world of fruit, so fresh, serene!

Serenity in a Bowl of Acai

In a bowl so round and bright,
Berries dancing, such delight.
With granola swirls, a crunchy cheer,
Breakfast comes, the fun is near.

Spoon dives deep, oh so slick,
Colors burst, it's quite the trick.
Taste bud party, feel the groove,
Who knew health could be a move?

Bananas smile, they jump around,
Mixed with honey, joy is found.
A scoop of laughter, take a chance,
In this bowl, we all will dance.

So let's rejoice with every bite,
Savor the joy, feel oh-so-right.
In this paradise, we're drawn,
Waking up feels like a song.

Starfruit Dreams on Velvet Waves

Star-shaped wonders, bright and bold,
Their shiny skins, a sight to behold.
Slice them up, a cosmic treat,
Fruit spaceship ready for a beat!

Juice drips down, oh what a splash,
Making drinks, oh what a bash!
On velvet waves, the laughter roars,
Surfing fruits on ocean shores.

Pineapple surfboards, coconut skies,
Every sip brings goofy sighs.
Under the sun, our giggles play,
Fruitful dreams take us away.

Let's build a castle of citrus bright,
With juicy walls, it feels just right.
In this kingdom, we all agree,
Life's just a game of fruity glee!

Midnight Harvest of Ripe Durian

Under the moon, a stinky prize,
Durian's scent, oh how it flies!
Open it up, the smell's no joke,
With every bite, it's a taste folks provoke.

Friends gather 'round, holding their nose,
What crazy fruit, nobody knows!
We laugh and cheer, the daring feast,
Is it perfume or an odd beast?

Creamy gold hosts a quirky flavor,
With every bite, our taste buds waver.
A midnight munch, adventures await,
This spiky delight, we can't underrate.

So bring on giggles as we dive in,
In this durian challenge, let's grin!
With laughter shared and snacks extreme,
Midnight's finest, a wacky dream!

The Garden of Maracuja Musings

In a garden lush, the passion fruit grows,
With yellow hues that glow and pose.
Juicy treasures tucked away tight,
Nature's candy, a sheer delight.

With each scoop, a burst of zest,
Who'd have guessed it's truly the best?
Giggling seeds in fruity pools,
Sipping dreams, oh, we are fools!

Maracuja cocktails, exotic flair,
Pour it up high, let's dance and stare.
Sipping slow, we start to sway,
It's a fruity fiesta, hip-hip-hooray!

Let's dig in deep, with silly grins,
A fruity adventure where laughter spins.
In the garden, we lose all strife,
With passion fruit, we spice up life!

Cacao's Velvet Touch

In a land where chocolate rains,
Beans dance on lush green plains.
With every bite, a giggle grows,
As sweet surprise is what one knows.

The laughter peels like sticky bars,
And cocoa dreams reach up to stars.
Each nibble wraps you in delight,
Like velvet hugs wrapped up so tight.

A chocolate river flows with glee,
Where squirrels surf on creamy sea.
Berries bounce on frothy waves,
As laughter echoes through the caves.

Oh, melt my heart with every taste,
In this place, there's no time to waste.
Cacao whispers, "Join the fun!"
And joy erupts with every run.

Under the Breadfruit Moon

Where breadfruits glow like golden cheese,
And giggling bananas sway in the breeze.
Laughter ripens on every vine,
As we dance with joy, feeling fine.

The moon's a pie, all flaky and bright,
Casting shadows that tickle at night.
Mangoes plot a juicy charade,
While echoed giggles never fade.

Coconuts roll with giddy flair,
As we all break into a dare.
"Who can juggle the fruits we have?"
The breadfruit moon winks and laughs.

With every bite, a funny dance,
Silly fruit leads us in a trance.
Underneath the starlit glow,
Our hearts are light, our joys will flow.

Dreams of a Citrus Paradise

Lemons laugh with zesty zest,
While oranges wear their Sunday best.
Grapefruits gossip, sweet and sour,
As they chat in a citrus tower.

Tangerines tumble, rolling wild,
Like silly kids, they're free and mild.
Limes lime-light as they take the stage,
Dancing away like they're of age.

Sun-kissed fruits in a vibrant show,
Juicy laughter, a constant flow.
Every bite's a burst of cheer,
Citrus dreams ring bright and clear.

Lemonade rivers, fresh and bold,
With sugar splash, a wonder to behold.
Swinging on vines, we'll twirl and sway,
In this orchard, we'll laugh all day!

Memories of Melodious Mangoes

Mangoes hum a gentle tune,
Swinging under the lazy moon.
Their golden skins, a joy to see,
With sweetened whispers, they call to me.

Each slice a note in fruity song,
As sticky fingers can't go wrong.
They dance and sway, so bright and free,
In this grove, there's much to be!

Melodies of summer breeze,
As laughter drifts like honeyed cheese.
With each ripe bite, a tune unfolds,
Mangoes share their tales so bold.

Memories burst like sunshine drops,
A fruity chorus that never stops.
In the land where laughter sings,
The mangoes sway on joyful wings.

The Celebration of Citrus

Lemon's laughter fills the air,
Lime's sweet giggles, everywhere!
Oranges bounce in joyful glee,
A zesty dance, come join, you see!

Grapefruits wear their sassy hats,
While mandarins sing with the cats.
In this party, zest is key,
So let's all sip on lemonade tea!

Pineapples spin with bright delight,
Wear sunglasses, oh what a sight!
Kiwi jokes that never fall flat,
Their fuzzy charm: imagine that!

With fruity pies and punch galore,
We'll laugh and play, and grab some more.
This citrus bash will never end,
A fruity hug from every friend!

Exploring Lychee Landscapes

In fields of pink, the lychees grow,
Each one a secret, much to know.
Bouncing around with jelly-like flair,
A squishy surprise, beyond compare!

With each soft bite, a giggle emerges,
Juicy laughter that never purges.
Their fruity giggles fill the breeze,
Exploring flavors, Oh, what a tease!

In dreams of lychee, we take a flight,
Through swirling skies, a fruity delight.
Clouds like candy, skies like cream,
Floating together in a sweet dream!

Adventures await in every pink nook,
Grab your spoon and let's take a look!
With lychee treasures, tales unfold,
Our playful hearts, we must uphold!

Fragrances of Frangipani

Frangipani whispers in the breeze,
A playful fragrance, oh, if you please!
With petals soft, like laughter's dance,
They twirl around, given the chance!

In sunny patches of creamy delight,
Dreams of sweetness take off in flight.
Bees start buzzing, join in the fun,
Tickle the flowers, oh what a run!

The scent of mischief fills the air,
With blooms that giggle, everywhere.
Let's frolic through this fragrant land,
Where petals lead, hand in hand!

Dancing beneath the bright blue skies,
Frangipani—the prankster's prize!
In this garden of whimsy, we roam,
With joy in our hearts, we feel at home!

Nectar Dreams on Golden Sails

On waves of honey, dreams set sail,
With nectar's sweetness, we'll never fail.
Mangoes cheer from the sunny shore,
As we taste the treasures, craving more!

Melons wear crowns, oh look at them grin,
A fruity regatta ready to win.
Under the sun, laughter prevails,
As we float on fruits with golden sails!

Papaya pirates, they sing and sway,
Guiding our ship through sparkling spray.
Tropical vibes, a merry parade,
In juicy waves, let's dance unafraid!

So grab your slice of this fruity fun,
Under the moon, when day is done.
With nectar dreams and laughter so bright,
We'll sail forever into the night!

Lush Lounges of Lychee

In a grove where lychees laugh,
Sipping dreams from juicy halves,
They wear shades made of berry bliss,
Winking bids not to be missed.

With each bite, a giggle spills,
Like fruity jokes that give us chills,
Avocados dance in the breeze,
While bananas chuckle from the trees.

Passionfruit flirts with a melon sweet,
In a hammock where all friends meet,
Swaying softly, they tell a tale,
Of kooky harvests and fruity sail.

Oh, the laughter peels like ripe kiwi,
As we feast with glee, our hearts feel free,
Lush lounges call, let's stay awhile,
With fruits that tease and make us smile.

Aroma of Hibiscus

Hibiscus wafts a scent so bold,
Making elephants wear hats of gold,
They tiptoe near, all shy and sweet,
Juggling pineapples as their treat.

A floral brew in a teacup sat,
With giggling berries, and where's the cat?
Each sip's a charming, fragrant prank,
While honey grapes fill up a tank.

Mango, in a tutu, starts to sway,
While guavas cheer and shout, "Hooray!"
Coconuts laugh, spilling their tea,
A merry picnic comes to be.

All the blooms join in the cheer,
With lively dances, oh so dear,
In this garden of colors, bright,
Laughter ripples in morning light.

Enchanted Orchard

In an orchard where dreams take flight,
Fruit fairies twirl, such a sight,
Where apples giggle and pears entwine,
Whispering secrets on the vine.

Rambutan wears a silly grin,
While cherries play tag, eager to win,
Peaches throw confetti in the air,
As nectarines dance without a care.

Kiwifruit wearing a wizard's hat,
Casting spells, can you believe that?
They shimmer in sunlight, gleeful and bright,
Turning ordinary days into delight.

The enchanted orchard, full of glee,
Is where fruit dreams come to be,
With laughter echoing through the tree,
Join the fun, come dance with me!

Maracuja Moonbeam

In the night, maracuja glows,
As silly shadows prance and pose,
With jellybeans dancing on the ground,
Where laughter lifts the heart around.

Beneath the stars, bananas sway,
Whispering dreams in a quirky way,
Papayas donned in shades of pink,
Giggle and chatter, oh, how they think!

A moonbeam kiss, a playful tease,
As mangoes dance in the warm breeze,
While custard apples roll in delight,
Creating mayhem in the warm night.

Maracuja's laugh, a joyous sound,
With fruity friends that dance around,
So come and join this moony scheme,
Find your joy in the fruity dream!

www.ingramcontent.com/pod-product-compliance
Lightning Source LLC
Chambersburg PA
CBHW070320120526
44590CB00017B/2756

The Passionate Peach

Oh, the peach is a flirty one,
With fuzz and blush, it's having fun!
Wobbly and ripe, it takes the stage,
So sweet and juicy, oh what a rage!

It whispers secrets, soft and low,
As we bite in, our faces glow.
With every chew, it's pure romance,
Who knew a fruit could make us dance?

A splash of juice, down goes the shirt,
Oops! A peach faceplant, oh does it hurt!
But giggles bubble, laughter rings,
From fruity slips, joy surely springs!

So grab a peach, it's a lively date,
With nectar drips, we celebrate.
In each sweet bite, let's take our chance,
For fruity love is the best romance!

Melon Mirage

In the summer sun, a melon appears,
With stripes and spots, it draws good cheers.
A fruity illusion in green and gold,
Open it up, let the magic unfold!

Wobbling slices, a giggle they bring,
A splash of juice, a mouth-watering zing.
It rolls and tumbles, all over the place,
A slippery gem, can't keep up the pace!

With laughter loud, we take our aim,
Spitting seeds is part of the game.
Who can hit the target and win?
Victory tastes like a fruity grin!

So let's celebrate in this fruity spree,
The mirage is real, come join with glee.
For every slice holds a fun surprise,
Melon magic beneath sunny skies!